Living for Christ in a Cynical World

Living for Christ in a Cynical World

by
John MacArthur, Jr.

"GRACE TO YOU"
P.O. Box 4000
Panorama City, CA 91412

©1991 by
JOHN F. MACARTHUR, JR.

ISBN: 0-8024-5388-0

1 2 3 4 5 Printing/LC/Year 95 94 93 92 91

Printed in the United States of America

Contents

1. Godly Living   7
   Tape GC 60-23—1 Peter 2:11-12

2. Submission to Civil Authority—Part 1   17
   Tape GC 60-24—1 Peter 2:13*a-b*

3. Submission to Civil Authority—Part 2   25
   Tape GC 60-25—1 Peter 2:13*c*-17

4. Submission in the Workplace—Part 1   35
   Tape GC 60-26—1 Peter 2:18-19*a*

5. Submission in the Workplace—Part 2   45
   Tape GC 60-27—1 Peter 2:19-23

6. How to Win Your Unbelieving Spouse   55
   Tape GC 60-31—1 Peter 3:1-7

   Scripture Index   65

   Topical Index   69

These Bible studies are taken from messages delivered by Pastor-Teacher John MacArthur, Jr., at Grace Community Church in Sun Valley, California. These messages have been combined into a 6-tape album titled *Living for Christ in a Cynical World*. You may purchase this series either in an attractive vinyl cassette album or as individual cassettes. To purchase these tapes, request the album *Living for Christ in a Cynical World*, or ask for the tapes by their individual GC numbers. Please consult the current price list; then send your order, making your check payable to:

"GRACE TO YOU"
P.O. Box 4000
Panorama City, CA 91412

Or call the following toll-free number:
1-800-55-GRACE

1

Godly Living

Outline

Introduction
A. The Need for Godliness
  1. A key passage
  2. A key phrase
B. The Importance of Godliness

Lesson
I. Godly Discipline (v. 11)
  A. Who Is Responsible (v. 11*a*)
  B. What the Responsibility Is (v. 11*b*)
II. Godly Behavior (v. 12)
  A. It Refutes Slanderous Accusations
  B. It Leads Others to Salvation
    1. God's visitation in the Old Testament
    2. God's visitation in the New Testament

Conclusion

Introduction

A. The Need for Godliness

The believers Peter wrote to were facing severe persecution. That persecution included slander and false accusations. The believers needed to know how to handle such a situation.

1. A key passage

In response Peter wrote, "Beloved, I urge you as aliens and strangers to abstain from fleshly lusts, which wage war against the soul. Keep your behavior excellent among the Gentiles, so that in the thing in which they slander you as evildoers, they may on account of your good deeds, as they observe them, glorify God in the day of visitation.

"Submit yourselves for the Lord's sake to every human institution, whether to a king as the one in authority, or to governors as sent by him for the punishment of evildoers and the praise of those who do right. For such is the will of God that by doing right you may silence the ignorance of foolish men. Act as free men, and do not use your freedom as a covering for evil, but use it as bondslaves of God. Honor all men; love the brotherhood, fear God, honor the king.

"Servants, be submissive to your masters with all respect, not only to those who are good and gentle, but also to those who are unreasonable. For this finds favor, if for the sake of conscience toward God a man bears up under sorrows when suffering unjustly. For what credit is there if, when you sin and are harshly treated, you endure it with patience? But if when you do what is right and suffer for it you patiently endure it, this finds favor with God" (1 Pet. 2:11-20).

2. A key phrase

The key phrase of that entire passage is in verse 15: "By doing right you may silence the ignorance of foolish men." The Greek term translated "silence" (*phimoō*) pictures muzzling an animal. It speaks of silencing an adversary by disproving his accusations. The accusations come from "the ignorance of foolish men." Their criticism against God's people is both ignorant and foolish. The way of silencing their unfounded criticism is "by doing right." Doing right means living a godly life. That's the believer's most effective tool for evangelism.

Our conduct is not only the critic's greatest point of attack, but also our greatest point of vulnerability. Scandalous conduct fuels the fires of criticism, but godly living extinguishes them. Commentator Robert

Leighton wrote, "When a Christian walks irreprovably, his enemies have no where to fasten their teeth on him, but are forced to gnaw their own malignant tongues. As it secures the godly, thus to stop the lying mouths of foolish men, so it is as painful to them to be thus stopped, as muzzling is to beasts, and it punishes their malice. And this is a wise Christian's way, instead of impatiently fretting at the mistakes or wilful miscensures of men, to keep still on his calm temper of mind, and upright course of life, and silent innocence; this, as a rock, breaks the waves into foam that roar about it" (*Commentary on First Peter* [Grand Rapids: Kregel, 1972 repr.], p. 195).

One skeptic offered this challenge to Christians: "Show me your redeemed life and I'll be inclined to believe in your Redeemer." The great Scottish preacher Alexander MacLaren said, "The world takes its notions of God, most of all, from the people who say that they belong to God's family. They read us a great deal more than they read the Bible. They see us; they only hear about Jesus Christ" (*First and Second Peter and First John* [N. Y.: Eaton and Maines, 1910], p. 105).

The foundation of evangelism is not so much what we say, but what we do. As is often said, "Actions speak louder than words." Christ put it this way: "Let your light shine before men in such a way that they may see your good works, and glorify your Father who is in heaven" (Matt. 5:16).

B. The Importance of Godliness

Peter wrote to believers who were experiencing difficult circumstances. They had been dispersed in various hostile, pagan lands and were being persecuted for their faith (1 Pet. 1:1; 4:12). Peter reminded them that they were very special to God and the recipients of divine privileges (2:9-10). In light of that, they were to live in godliness. That's because a spiritually transformed life attracts unbelievers to Christ and lays a platform of credibility for what we say. Christ is our example to follow because He lived a perfectly righteous life (2:21-25).

Peter identified believers as foreigners (2:11-12), citizens (vv. 13-17), and servants (vv. 18-20). All believers fall into those roles. They are three arenas where the lost observe our lives. How we live certainly has an impact on the lost.

9

A believing wife, for example, can win her unbelieving husband to Christ through her godly, respectful behavior (3:1). And all of us, whether at home, school, or work, should live godly lives because it's God's way of silencing our critics. Second Peter 2:11-12 tells us how to live that way.

Lesson

I. GODLY DISCIPLINE (v. 11)

"Beloved, I urge you as aliens and strangers to abstain from fleshly lusts, which wage war against the soul."

A. Who Is Responsible (v. 11a)

"Beloved, I urge you as aliens and strangers."

Peter used the term "beloved" (Gk., *agapētos*) eight times in his two letters to identify the believers and remind them that they were the objects of God's great love. He was urging them to reciprocate that love through obedience. Peter wrote that the believers were not only beloved but also "aliens and strangers." He identified them as such because as believers their citizenship was in heaven (Phil. 3:20). We're not to love the world since God has taken us out of that kingdom of darkness and placed us into the kingdom of God's Son (cf. 1 John 2:15-17). Our heavenly citizenship is a privilege, but the price of that privilege is to live by God's standard, not the world's.

The Greek term translated "aliens" (*paroikos*) literally means "alongside the house." It refers to someone living as a foreigner in a land. The term "strangers" (Gk., *parepidēmos*) refers to a visitor making a brief stay, a sojourner passing through a country, or a traveler moving around within a land. In this life we live alongside unbelievers who have different beliefs, values, and morals. We "do not have a lasting city, but we are seeking the city which is to come" (Heb. 13:14). We know that our true home is in heaven.

B. What the Responsibility Is (v. 11b)

"Abstain from fleshly lusts, which wage war against the soul."

10

The believer is "to abstain from fleshly lusts." The Greek term translated "abstain" (*apechō*) literally means "to hold away from." The phrase "fleshly lusts" refers to the strong cravings of our sinful nature. Although we have a transformed life in Christ, we still remain in a spiritual battle, fighting against desires that would lead to sin (cf. Rom. 7:14-25).

Yielding to fleshly lusts manifests itself in various ways: "immorality, impurity, sensuality, idolatry, sorcery, enmities, strife, jealousy, outbursts of anger, disputes, dissensions, factions, envying, drunkenness, [and] carousing" (Gal. 5:19-21). In contrast to that we are to long for God's Word and offer spiritual sacrifices (1 Pet. 2:2, 5). Because there is a constant spiritual battle between contrasting desires, believers eagerly wait for the redemption of our bodies (Rom. 8:23). Only then will we enjoy perfect righteousness.

The believer is to stay away from the strong cravings of his sinful nature, "which wage war against the soul" (1 Pet. 2:11). The Greek term translated "which" (*haitines*) refers to the nature of something. By their very nature, strong fleshly desires fight against the soul. James 4:1 puts it this way: "What causes fights and quarrels among you? Don't they come from your desires that battle within you?" (NIV*; cf. 1:14-15).

The term "soul" simply refers to what's inside a person. When God created man, He fashioned him into a living soul, or being (Gen. 2:7). The strong desires of our sinful nature "wage war" (Gk., *strateuō*) against the soul. The verb speaks of carrying on a long-term military campaign, not a skirmish or one-time battle. In 1 Peter 2:11 fleshly lusts are personified as an army of rebels who intend to capture, enslave, and destroy the human soul. The verb implies not just antagonism, but constant and malicious aggression. Fleshly lusts wage an incessant search-and-destroy mission against us.

We are not to surrender to fleshly desires or give them any advantage in their assault (cf. 1 Pet. 4:1-3). Galatians 5:16 says that the key to spiritual victory is walking by the Spirit. In 2 Corinthians 10:4-5 the apostle Paul says, "The weapons of our warfare are not of the flesh, but

New International Version.

11

divinely powerful for the destruction of fortresses. We are destroying speculations and every lofty thing raised up against the knowledge of God, and we are taking every thought captive to the obedience of Christ."

II. GODLY BEHAVIOR (v. 12)

"Keep your behavior excellent among the Gentiles, so that in the thing in which they slander you as evildoers, they may on account of your good deeds, as they observe them, glorify God in the day of visitation."

Godliness begins with inner spiritual discipline and then is reflected outwardly in one's behavior. "Behavior" (Gk., *anastrophē*) refers to one's daily conduct or manner of life. The Greek term translated "excellent" (*kalos*) speaks of something that is winsome, attractive, fine, or noble. It is goodness in the purest and highest sense. The believer is to manifest good conduct before the "Gentiles" (Gk., *ethnos*, from which we derive the English word *ethnic*). It's a general reference to the lost world (cf. 1 Cor. 5:1; 12:2; 3 John 7). The lost should be able to see consistent good behavior in the life of any true Christian.

A. It Refutes Slanderous Accusations

First Peter 2:12 says believers will be slandered as "evildoers." That refers to very wicked people worthy of severe punishment (cf. v. 14; 4:15). In Peter's day the lost used that term to heap extreme verbal abuse and contempt against Christians, whom they hated, despised, and mistrusted (cf. Acts 17:6; 28:22). The lost accused Christians of insurrection against the Roman government, cannibalism, and immorality. They were also accused of damaging trade and social progress, ruining family life, leading slaves into rebellion, and hating people. The believer is to refute such slander and false accusations by his or her "good deeds" (1 Pet. 2:12).

B. It Leads Others to Salvation

By seeing the believer's good deeds over a period of time, some unbelievers will "glorify God in the day of visitation" (1 Pet. 2:12). The "day of visitation" refers to a visit from God.

12

1. God's visitation in the Old Testament

   In the Old Testament God visited man for two basic reasons: blessing or judgment. The blessing was often some form of national deliverance from oppression.

   a) Isaiah 10:3—The Lord said to the nation Israel, "What will ye do in the day of visitation, and in the desolation which shall come from far?" (KJV*). The Lord was going to visit Israel with judgment because of its sin.

   b) Genesis 50:24—"Joseph said unto his brethren, 'I die: and God will surely visit you, and bring you out of this land'" (KJV). Joseph was certain that God would deliver His people from Egyptian bondage.

   c) Jeremiah 27:22—The Lord said, "They shall be carried to Babylon, and they shall be there until the day I visit them. . . . Then I will bring them back and restore them to this place." The Lord was promising to deliver His people from the Babylonian Captivity.

   d) 1 Samuel 2:21—"The Lord visited Hannah; and she conceived and gave birth to three sons and two daughters. And the boy Samuel grew before the Lord." God visited Hannah and blessed her with a child.

2. God's visitation in the New Testament

   Whereas God's visitation in the Old Testament generally refers to judgment or blessing, it specifically refers to redemption or salvation in the New Testament.

   a) Luke 1:68—Zechariah, the father of John the Baptist, said, "Blessed be the Lord God of Israel, for He has visited us and accomplished redemption for His people."

   b) Luke 7:16—"God has visited His people!" That was the people's response after Christ raised a widow's son from the dead.

*King James Version.

13

c) Luke 19:44—In weeping over Jerusalem, Christ said, "You did not recognize the time of your visitation." He mourned that Israel as a whole failed to realize the salvation He would provide.

Certainly "the day of visitation" in 1 Peter 2:12 refers to salvation. When the Lord visits the unbeliever and opens his heart, that person will remember observing the godly behavior of faithful Christians and respond in saving faith. That kind of response glorifies God.

Conclusion

During World War II, missionaries Herb and Ruth Clingen and their young son spent three years in a Japanese prison camp in the Philippines. In his diary Herb recorded that their captors murdered, tortured, and starved to death many of their fellow prisoners. The camp commandant, Konishi, was hated and feared more than the others. Herb writes, "Konishi found an inventive way to abuse us even more. He *increased* the food ration but gave us *palay*—unhusked rice. Eating the rice with its razor-sharp outer shell would cause intestinal bleeding that would kill us in hours. We had no tools to remove the husks, and doing the job manually—by pounding the grain or rolling it with a heavy stick—consumed more calories than the rice would supply. It was a death sentence for all internees" (Herb and Ruth Clingen, "Song of Deliverance," *Masterpiece* [Spring 1989], p. 12).

Before death could claim their lives, however, General Douglas MacArthur and his forces liberated them from captivity. That very day Konishi had planned to gun down all the remaining prisoners. Years later Herb and Ruth "learned that Konishi had been found working as a grounds keeper at a Manila golf course. He was put on trial for his war crimes and hanged. Before his execution he professed conversion to Christianity, saying he had been deeply affected by the testimony of the Christian missionaries he had persecuted" ("Song of Deliverance," p. 13). When God graciously visited Konishi with salvation, that one-time torturer remembered the godly behavior of missionaries he once persecuted. Their example became the unspoken means of Konishi's salvation.

Focusing on the Facts

1. What is the key phrase in 1 Peter 2:11-20 (see p. 8)?
2. What does "silence" speak of in 1 Peter 2:11 (see p. 8)?
3. What is the way to silence unfounded criticism (1 Pet. 2:15; see p. 8)?
4. What is the believer's most effective tool for evangelism (see p. 8)?
5. What is the critic's greatest point of attack and our greatest point of vulnerability (see p. 8)?
6. What were the circumstances of the believers to whom Peter wrote (see p. 9)?
7. A spiritually transformed life lays a platform of _____ (see p. 9).
8. Whose example of righteousness should we follow (1 Pet. 2:21-25; see p. 9)?
9. Why does Peter identify believers as "aliens and strangers" (1 Pet. 2:11)? How should that affect your conduct (1 John 2:15-17; see p. 10)?
10. What do "fleshly lusts" refer to (1 Pet. 2:11; see p. 11)?
11. How do fleshly lusts manifest themselves (Gal. 5:19-21; see p. 11)?
12. How are fleshly lusts personified in 1 Peter 2:11 (see p. 11)?
13. What is the key to victory in our fight against fleshly lusts (Gal. 5:16; see p. 12)?
14. How is inner spiritual discipline reflected (see p. 12)?
15. What does "the day of visitation" refer to in the New Testament (1 Pet. 2:12; see pp. 13-14)?
16. When God visits an unbeliever and opens his heart, what will that person remember and how will he respond (see p. 14)?

Pondering the Principles

1. Puritan Richard Baxter offered this practical advice about abstaining from fleshly lusts: "As a man that goeth with a candle among gunpowder, or near thatch, should never be careless, because he goeth in continual danger; so you . . . should remember that you carry fire and gunpowder still about you, and are never out of danger while you have such an enemy to watch" (*The Practical Works of Richard Baxter*, vol. 1 [Ligonier, Pa.: Soli Deo Gloria, 1990], p. 55). Exercise inner discipline. "Put on the Lord Jesus Christ, and make no provision for the flesh in regard to its lusts" (Rom. 13:14).

2. Look up the following verses and write out the principles they teach about godly living:

- 1 Timothy 2:1-2

- 1 Timothy 4:7

- 1 Timothy 6:10-11

- Titus 2:12

- 2 Peter 1:3-8

2

Submission to Civil Authority—Part 1

Outline

Introduction

Lesson
I.   The Command for Submission (v. 13*a*)
II. The Motive for Submission (v. 13*b*)
   A. To Obey the Lord
   B. To Imitate the Lord
   C. To Glorify the Lord
     1. By obeying civil laws
     2. By obeying God's Word
     3. By fighting with spiritual weapons
       a) God's Word
       b) Prayer

Conclusion

Introduction

Those who call themselves Christians sometimes harm the testimony of true Christianity by the way they behave toward civil authorities. Although believers are to set their affections on heaven, they are also to be godly citizens in society. That's why the apostle Peter said, "Submit yourselves for the Lord's sake to every human institution" (1 Pet. 2:13). He was commanding believers to respect civil authority.

Peter wrote to believers living under a pagan, hostile, and anti-Semitic Roman government. Many assumed that Christianity was nothing more than a sect of Judaism. Believers became the

17

objects of slander closely associated with malicious rumors that had already been circulating about the Jewish people. Apion, for example, made this false accusation: "In the reign of Antiochus Epiphanes, the Jews every year fattened a Greek, and having solemnly offered him up as a sacrifice on a fixed day in a certain forest, ate his entrails and swore eternal hostility to the Greeks" (cited by William Barclay in *The Letters of James and Peter*, rev. ed. [Philadelphia: Westminster, 1976], p. 202).

Believers were also accused of insurrection against Rome and all human authority. The Jewish religious leaders used that charge against Christ (cf. John 19:15). Believers were also accused of being atheists because they refused to worship pagan gods, including Caesar. They were accused of cannibalism because their enemies distorted the teaching of Christ and Paul regarding Communion (cf. John 6:53; 1 Cor. 10:16).

Believers were also accused of immorality. Long before Freud spoke of the Oedipus complex, pagans accused Christians of having incestuous relationships with one another simply because the believers referred to one another as brothers and sisters in Christ. The scriptural injunction to "greet one another with a holy kiss" was likewise maligned.

In addition, believers were accused of damaging trade in the idol-making business (Acts 19:21-41). They were accused of destroying family life, since homes were often divided when some family members became Christians, but others did not. They were accused of fostering slave rebellion, since a believing slave received new life and dignity in Christ. They were accused of hating people because they wouldn't adopt the world's ways.

Believers are to respond to such slander and hostility with godly living (1 Pet. 2:12; see pp. 10-14). That silences the critics, leaves no justification for false charges, and attracts unbelievers to Christ. Today society continues to be hostile toward Christianity. Although it is intolerant of truth and righteousness, we are to live as godly citizens and obey our civil authorities because that's what 1 Peter 2:13 teaches us to do.

Lesson

I. THE COMMAND FOR SUBMISSION (v. 13*a*)

"Submit yourselves."

The Greek term translated "submit yourselves" (*hupotassō*) is a military word that pictures a soldier under the rank of a commanding officer. The command could be translated, "Put yourselves in an attitude of submission." The ancient world tended to associate that attitude with cowards and weaklings, but God's Word teaches that submission to civil authority is the divine and right way to live.

A. Proverbs 24:21—"Fear the Lord and the king; do not associate with those who are given to change; for their calamity will rise suddenly, and who knows the ruin that comes from both of them?" God's people are to respect both divine and human authority, being careful not to ally themselves with troublemakers or insurrectionists.

B. Jeremiah 29:7—In Babylon the Jewish captives were in a pagan land ruled by an evil king. But the Lord said to His people, "Seek the welfare of the city where I have sent you into exile, and pray to the Lord on its behalf; for in its welfare you will have welfare." The Hebrew term translated "welfare" (*shalom*) means "peace." God's people were to pray for peace in the land and seek its welfare by building houses, planting gardens, and rearing godly families (v. 6). They were to rest in His sovereign control of the situation and not take matters into their own hands (vv. 8-14).

C. Romans 13:1-2—"Let every person be in subjection to the governing authorities. For there is no authority except from God, and those which exist are established by God. Therefore he who resists authority has opposed the ordinance of God; and they who have opposed will receive condemnation upon themselves." Even though slavery, physical abuse, murder, and immorality dominated Roman society and government, believers were to submit to civil authority because it was divinely ordained.

D. Matthew 22:21—Christ said, "Render to Caesar the things that are Caesar's." Believers are to pay whatever taxes they owe to the government.

II. THE MOTIVE FOR SUBMISSION (v. 13*b*)

"For the Lord's sake."

A. To Obey the Lord

The Lord has ordained civil authority (Rom. 13:1-7). So when a believer submits himself to it, he is obeying the Lord. When civil authorities say, "Do this," and it doesn't violate the teaching of God's Word, we should obey. God's kingdom doesn't benefit from disobedience.

We are to acknowledge God's control in all situations, not be troublemakers or lawbreakers. That's illustrated by what the Lord told the nation of Judah: "I will regard as good the captives of Judah, whom I have sent out of this place into the land of the Chaldeans. For I will set My eyes on them for good, and I will bring them again to this land; and I will build them up and not overthrow them, and I will plant them and not pluck them up. And I will give them a heart to know Me, for I am the Lord; and they will be My people, and I will be their God, for they will return to Me with their whole heart" (Jer. 24:5-7). Judah was not to rebel against its captors but accept its situation as part of God's sovereign plan.

In his book *A Biblical View of Civil Government* Bible teacher Robert Culver wrote, "God alone has sovereign rights. . . . Democratic theory is no less unscriptural than divine right monarchy. By whatever means men come to positions of rulership—by dynastic descent, aristocratic family connection, plutocratic material resources, or by democratic election, 'there is no power but of God' (Rom. 13:1). Furthermore, civil government is an instrument, not an end. Men are proximate ends, but only God is ultimate end. The state owns neither its citizens nor their properties, minds, bodies, or children. All of these belong to their Creator-God, who has never given to the state rights of eminent domain" ([Chicago: Moody, 1974], p. 47). God is the ultimate authority who calls us to obey His divine law.

B. To Imitate the Lord

When the believer submits to civil authority, he not only obeys the Lord but also imitates the example Christ purposely left us (1 Pet. 2:21). When reviled by His enemies, He "did not revile in return; while suffering, He uttered no threats, but kept entrusting Himself to Him who judges righteously" (v. 23). Although Christ lived under the pagan Roman government, He didn't attack its rulers. He never led a protest march against Roman or Jewish authorities. Even though His own trial was a mockery, He did not lash out against the authorities.

Instead of concerning Himself with earthly matters, Christ spoke only of God's kingdom, calling sinners to repentance and inviting them to come to Him (cf. Matt. 11:28-30). He entrusted Himself to God, bearing our sins on the cross at the hands of both Roman and Jewish authorities.

C. To Glorify the Lord

1. By obeying civil laws

God is honored when the lost observe Christians characterized by submission, virtue, kindness, graciousness, and humility. Educator and minister Robert Haldane well said, "The people of God . . . ought to consider resistance to the government under which they live as a very awful crime" (*Commentary on Romans* [Grand Rapids: Kregel, 1988], p. 587). Such resistance is often manifested in anger and hatred, both of which are obvious sins.

It's sad to see those who name Christ defy the very government He has ordained. Romans 13:3-5 says, "Rulers are not a cause of fear for good behavior, but for evil. Do you want to have no fear of authority? Do what is good, and you will have praise from the same; for it is a minister of God to you for good. But if you do what is evil, be afraid; for it does not bear the sword for nothing; for it is a minister of God, an avenger who brings wrath upon the one who practices evil. Wherefore it is necessary to be in subjection, not only because of wrath, but also for conscience' sake."

When civil authorities uphold law and order, they function as God's ministers, fulfilling a God-ordained role of keeping order in society. If a person obeys the law, he has no reason to fear. But if he breaks it, he should fear, because God has ordained civil authorities to punish lawbreakers. That we're to submit "for conscience' sake" means we're to do it because it's right.

2. By obeying God's Word

The one exception is if civil authorities tell us to do something that would violate God's Word. In Acts 4:18

the Sanhedrin commanded Peter and John "not to speak or teach at all in the name of Jesus." But Peter and John said, "Whether it is right in the sight of God to give heed to you rather than to God, you be the judge; for we cannot stop speaking what we have seen and heard" (vv. 19-20; cf. 5:29). As believers we must stand for the Lord and be willing to suffer the consequences.

But we must be careful not to go beyond the teaching of God's Word. When the authorities put Paul and Silas in stocks for preaching the Word in Philippi, the two sang hymns of praise (Acts 16:23-25). They certainly weren't rebelling against the authorities or resisting arrest. The Lord used their submissiveness and godliness to lead others to salvation (vv. 31-34).

3. By fighting with spiritual weapons

Paul realized that we as Christians are engaged in spiritual warfare: "Though we walk in the flesh, we do not war according to the flesh, for the weapons of our warfare are not of the flesh, but divinely powerful for the destruction of fortresses. We are destroying speculations and every lofty thing raised up against the knowledge of God, and we are taking every thought captive to the obedience of Christ" (2 Cor. 10:3-5).

The Greek term translated "weapons" (*hoplon*) refers to instruments of war. We are to fight with divinely powered spiritual weapons, not man-made ones. "Destruction" (*kathairesis*) means "to tear down." Our spiritual weapons effectively tear down massive strongholds of sin and Satan such as "speculations" (*logismos*) and "lofty [things]" (*hupsōma*), which refer to human thoughts and reasoning. The term "every" shows the tearing down to be comprehensive. Verses 3-5 picture an army moving against a city and tearing down everything in its path.

Believers are to be "taking every thought captive to the obedience of Christ" (v. 5). That pictures a soldier using a spear to take prisoners of war. All thoughts that oppose God are to bow in obedience to Christ. As believers we have two prominent spiritual weapons.

a) God's Word

Ephesians 6:17 calls us to arm ourselves with God's Word. We are to preach God's Word with power and conviction, calling sinners to repentance. The preaching of God's Word is always effective (cf. Isa. 55:11).

b) Prayer

Another spiritual weapon is prayer. In 1 Timothy 2:1-2 Paul says, "I urge that entreaties and prayers, petitions and thanksgivings, be made on behalf of all men, for kings and all who are in authority, in order that we may lead a tranquil and quiet life in all godliness and dignity." Through prayer the lost hear the gospel and are saved (vv. 3-6).

Conclusion

The early church submitted itself to the pagan Roman government, realizing that God ordains civil authority. What about you? Will you honor and obey God and His Word by submitting to your civil authorities?

Focusing on the Facts

1. Although believers are to set their affections on heaven, they are also to be _____ _____ in society (see p. 17).
2. What does Proverbs 24:21 teach (see p. 19)?
3. How were the Jewish captives to behave toward the Babylonian government (Jer. 29:7-14; see p. 19)?
4. Why were believers to submit to the Roman government (Rom. 13:1-2; see p. 19)?
5. What does Matthew 22:21 teach (see p. 19)?
6. When a believer submits to civil authority, he is obeying the _____ (see p. 20).
7. What does Jeremiah 24:5-7 illustrate (see p. 20)?
8. What example does Christ leave us in 1 Peter 2:23 (see pp. 20-21)?
9. What did Robert Haldane call "a very awful crime" (see p. 21)?
10. When civil authorities uphold law and order, they function as _____ _____ (Rom. 13:4; see p. 21).

11. What does "for conscience' sake" mean in 1 Peter 2:13 (see p. 21)?
12. What does Acts 4:19-20 teach (see pp. 21-22)?
13. What must we be careful not to do? How is that illustrated in Acts 16:23-34 (see p. 22)?
14. Christians are engaged in _____ _____ (2 Cor. 10:3-5; see p. 22).
15. How effective are our spiritual weapons (2 Cor. 10:3-5; see pp. 22)?
16. What are two prominent spiritual weapons (see pp. 22-23)?

Pondering the Principles

1. Commentator John Brown wrote, "It is the duty of a Christian to yield obedience to all laws of the government under which he lives, that are not inconsistent with the law of God. When the human ordinance contradicts the Divine ordinance, requiring us to do what God forbids, or forbidding us to do what God requires, the rule is plain: 'We ought to obey God rather than man' [Acts 5:29]. Nothing short of this, however, can warrant a Christian to withhold obedience from a law of the government under which, in the providence of God, he is placed" (*Expository Discourses on 1 Peter* [Carlisle, Pa.: Banner of Truth, 1975], pp. 349-50). Evaluate your attitude toward civil authority. Does it agree with the teaching of God's Word? Ask the Lord to help you be submissive and respectful to the authorities. That way your life will honor the Lord and attract unbelievers to Christ.

2. We're to submit to civil authorities because it's the right thing to do. Robert Culver wrote, "The Christian serves his country, obeys its laws, and supports its rulers so far as a biblically informed conscience lets him, not out of servile fear or out of rigid dogmatic necessity, but because he knows it is right. Right (understood as expression of the will of the Creator-God) is ultimately the ground of all righteous action" (*Toward a Biblical View of Civil Government*, p. 256). By doing right you will "let your light shine before men in such a way that they may see your good works, and glorify your Father who is in heaven" (Matt. 5:16).

3

Submission to Civil Authority—Part 2

Outline

Introduction
A. The Example of Stephen
  1. His opposition
  2. His response
  3. His godliness
B. The Example of Christ

Review
I. The Command for Submission (v. 13a)
II. The Motive for Submission (v. 13b)

Lesson
III. The Extent of Submission (vv. 13c-14)
  A. To Unjust Authorities
  B. To All Authorities
IV. The Reason for Submission (v. 15)
V. The Attitude of Submission (v. 16)
VI. The Application of Submission (v. 17)
  A. To All Mankind
  B. To Christians
  C. To God
  D. To the Authorities

Introduction

Both Stephen and Christ illustrate what godly living is all about.

A. The Example of Stephen

1. His opposition

Stephen, a deacon in the early church, "was performing great wonders and signs among the people. But some men . . . rose up and argued with Stephen. And yet they were unable to cope with the wisdom and the Spirit with which he was speaking. Then they secretly induced men to say, 'We have heard him speak blasphemous words against Moses and against God.'

"And they stirred up the people, the elders and the scribes, and they came upon him and dragged him away, and brought him before the Council. And they put forward false witnesses who said, 'This man incessantly speaks against this holy place, and the Law; for we have heard him say that this Nazarene, Jesus, will destroy this place and alter the customs which Moses handed down to us'" (Acts 6:8-14).

2. His response

Stephen responded to their false accusations by giving an evangelistic message (7:2-50). In conclusion he said, "You men who are stiff-necked and uncircumcised in heart and ears are always resisting the Holy Spirit; you are doing just as your fathers did. Which one of the prophets did your fathers not persecute? And they killed those who had previously announced the coming of the Righteous One, whose betrayers and murderers you have now become; you who received the law as ordained by angels, and yet did not keep it" (vv. 51-53).

3. His godliness

When Stephen's enemies heard that, "they were cut to the quick, and they began gnashing their teeth at him. But being full of the Holy Spirit, he gazed intently into heaven and saw the glory of God, and Jesus standing at the right hand of God; and he said, 'Behold, I see the heavens opened up and the Son of Man standing at the right hand of God.' But they cried out with a loud voice, and covered their ears, and they rushed upon him with one impulse.

"And when they had driven him out of the city, they began stoning him, and the witnesses laid aside their robes at the feet of a young man named Saul. And they went on stoning Stephen as he called upon the Lord and said, 'Lord Jesus, receive my spirit!' And falling on his knees, he cried out with a loud voice, 'Lord, do not hold this sin against them!' And having said this, he fell asleep. And Saul [Paul] was in hearty agreement with putting him to death" (7:54—8:1).

Certainly Stephen's death left an indelible impression on Paul. Although there was no just reason for his execution, Stephen trusted God and forgave his enemies. I believe his godly testimony was a key factor in Paul's conversion. Stephen's example was similar to Christ's.

B. The Example of Christ

When Christ was reviled, "He did not revile in return; while suffering, He uttered no threats, but kept entrusting Himself to Him who judges righteously" (1 Pet. 2:23). He endured His suffering quietly and patiently, while praying for the forgiveness of His enemies (Luke 23:34). It's no wonder the Roman centurion said, "Truly this was the Son of God!" (Matt. 27:54).

When you undergo a trial, know that unbelievers are watching how you respond, and that will affect how they respond to the gospel. First Peter 2:12 says believers are to be godly, and that includes submitting to civil authorities (vv. 13-17).

Review

I. THE COMMAND FOR SUBMISSION (v. 13*a*; see pp. 18-19)

II. THE MOTIVE FOR SUBMISSION (v. 13*b*; see pp. 19-23)

Our motive for submitting to the authorities is to honor Christ. That's illustrated in Matthew 17: "Those who collected the two-drachma tax came to Peter, and said, 'Does your teacher not pay the two-drachma tax?' He said, 'Yes.'

And when he came into the house, Jesus spoke to him first, saying, 'What do you think, Simon? From whom do the kings of the earth collect customs or poll-tax, from their sons or from strangers?' And upon his saying, 'From strangers,' Jesus said to him, 'Consequently the sons are exempt. But, lest we give them offense, go to the sea, and throw in a hook, and take the first fish that comes up; and when you open its mouth, you will find a stater [a coin worth four drachmas]. Take that and give it to them for you and Me'" (vv. 24-27).

Although Christ was the Son of God, He nevertheless paid the Jewish Temple tax because He didn't want to offend others. Obeying the law presents righteousness in a tangible way to unbelievers and attracts them to the righteousness of Christ and salvation.

Lesson

III. THE EXTENT OF SUBMISSION (vv. 13c-14)

"To every human institution, whether to a king as the one in authority, or to governors as sent by him for the punishment of evildoers and the praise of those who do right."

The Greek noun translated "institution" (*ktisis*) and its related verb refer exclusively to products, activities, or enterprises of God, not man. For example, in Mark 13:19 it refers to God's work of creation and in 2 Corinthians 5:17 to His work of regeneration. Here in 1 Peter 2:13 it refers to what God has ordained, namely, civil government (cf. Rom. 13:1-7).

A. To Unjust Authorities

Believers are to submit to "every" governing authority, even unjust ones. God's Word specifies that there are unjust rulers.

1. Isaiah 3:1-2, 8—"The Lord God of hosts is going to remove from Jerusalem and Judah both supply and support, the whole supply of bread, and the whole supply of water; the mighty man and the warrior, the judge and the prophet, the diviner and the elder. . . . For Jerusalem has stumbled, and Judah has fallen, because their speech and their actions are against the Lord, to rebel against His glorious presence." God judged the nation because its rulers were evil.

2. Daniel 9:11-12—"All Israel has transgressed Thy law and turned aside, not obeying Thy voice; so the curse has been poured out on us, along with the oath which is written in the law of Moses the servant of God, for we have sinned against Him. Thus He has confirmed His words which He had spoken against us and against our rulers who ruled us, to bring on us great calamity; for under the whole heaven there has not been done anything like what was done to Jerusalem." The Hebrew phrase translated "rulers who ruled us" literally means "judges who judged us." Because the rulers were evil, God judged them.

3. Micah 7:2-3—"The godly person has perished from the land, and there is no upright person among men. All of them lie in wait for bloodshed; each of them hunts the other with a net. Concerning evil, both hands do it well. The prince asks, also the judge, for a bribe." Micah lived in an evil society that included corrupt judges, so he pleaded for God to execute justice (v. 9).

4. Romans 13:1—"Let every person be in subjection to the governing authorities." In Paul's day corrupt judges presided over the trials of persecuted believers.

Although many rulers were unjust in those days, God's people were not to take matters into their own hands. Instead they were to trust God, who has the sovereign right to rule as He pleases. Robert Culver wrote, "Churchmen whose Christian activism has taken mainly to placarding, marching, protesting, and shouting might well observe [Paul] first at prayer, then in counsel with his friends, and after that preaching in the homes and market places. When Paul came to be heard by the mighty, it was to defend his action as a preacher . . . of a way to heaven (see Acts 26:1-32; Rom. 1:9-10)" (*Toward a Biblical View of Civil Government* [Chicago: Moody, 1974], p. 262). If believers are persecuted or imprisoned, it should be for preaching righteousness, not defying civil law.

B. To All Authorities

We are to submit to all civil authorities, "whether to a king as the one in authority, or to governors" (1 Pet. 2:13-14). That means we are to submit to every level of leadership in government. "King" (Gk., *basileus*) refers to the person in charge. Back then the king was Nero. Although he was an evil man, his function as a king was divinely ordained. "Governors" (*hēgemōn*) refers to all officials under the king. Scripture makes no distinction between submitting to pagan kings and governors or to those who are righteous.

God ordains civil authority "for the punishment of evildoers and the praise of those who do right" (1 Pet. 2:14). Its primary function is to punish those who break the law and reward those who keep it. Romans 13:3 says it this way: "Rulers are not a cause of fear for good behavior, but for evil." Civil authorities are ministers of God who bear arms to punish evildoers (13:4). The police, for example, have guns to uphold law and order. Civil authorities not only punish lawbreakers but also recognize meritorious citizens with praise (13:3).

IV. THE REASON FOR SUBMISSION (v. 15)

"Such is the will of God that by doing right you may silence the ignorance of foolish men."

The Greek term translated "silence" (*phimoō*) means "to muzzle." Christ used the word in commanding a demon to be quiet (Mark 1:25) and the sea to be calm (4:39). "Doing right" means "to do good." The term "ignorance" (Gk., *agnōsia*) refers not to a lack of knowledge but to a willful, hostile rejection of the truth. The believer's critics are also "foolish." That refers to reckless thinking. God's will is that we silence our critics by our righteous conduct and good citizenship.

That's why Titus reminded believers "to be subject to rulers, to authorities, to be obedient, to be ready for every good deed, to malign no one, to be uncontentious, gentle, showing every consideration for all men" (Titus 3:1-2). Believers were to submit to a pagan government, knowing they had received God's kindness and love in salvation (vv. 4-5). The church is to be gentle, gracious, and obedient toward civil authorities, not retaliatory or rebellious.

The same is true of the church's leaders. An elder "must have a good reputation with those outside the church, so that he may not fall into reproach and the snare of the devil" (1 Tim. 3:7). Often the basis of the believer's reputation before the lost is how he conducts himself as a citizen. An impeccable and virtuous character gives credibility to one's witness and honors the Lord.

V. THE ATTITUDE OF SUBMISSION (v. 16)

"Act as free men, and do not use your freedom as a covering for evil, but use it as bondslaves of God."

We are no longer slaves to the world, sin, or Satan because we have been redeemed by the precious blood of Christ (1 Pet. 1:18-19). However, we are not to use that freedom "as a covering for evil" (2:16). "Covering" refers to a veil and "evil" to baseness. We are not to use our liberty in Christ as a license for sin. I've heard people say things such as, "I don't pay my taxes because I'm a citizen of heaven," and, "I don't obey trespass laws because everything belongs to my Father. All that's His is mine." That kind of reasoning is wrong.

Believers are free to obey and serve God, not themselves. First Corinthians 7:22 says, "He who was called in the Lord while a slave, is the Lord's freedman; likewise he who was called while free, is Christ's slave" (cf. Rom. 6:22). Galatians 5:13 says, "You were called to freedom, brethren; only do not turn your freedom into an opportunity for the flesh, but through love serve one another." Our citizenship in heaven and our freedom in Christ do not allow us to disobey civil law.

VI. THE APPLICATION OF SUBMISSION (v. 17)

"Honor all men; love the brotherhood, fear God, honor the king."

That verse specifies four parameters of submission.

A. To All Mankind

"All men" refers to humanity. Because all persons were made in the image of God (cf. James 3:9), all are to be shown respect. In the Roman Empire many slaves were deprived of their dignity as human beings, but believers aren't to treat anyone that way. Every person deserves respect, regardless of his or her race, color, religion, or status in society. We might not agree with what others believe or do, but we are to value them as God's creation.

B. To Christians

"Love the brotherhood" refers to love for other believers.

31

C. To God

To "fear God" is to trust God in all situations, no matter how difficult circumstances might be. We are to reverence Him as the sovereign God who works all things by His perfect and unrestricted will. Our fear of Him will restrain us from disobedience.

D. To the Authorities

To "honor the king" is to respect the ruling authorities or leaders. Proverbs 24:21-22 says, "Fear the Lord and the king; do not associate with those who are given to change; for their calamity will rise suddenly, and who knows the ruin that comes from both of them?" Both the Lord and the king will afflict the rebellious and disobedient.

Honoring all mankind, loving your brothers and sisters in Christ, fearing God, and respecting the authorities give credibility to your gospel witness. Are you willing to be that kind of citizen?

Focusing on the Facts

1. How did Stephen respond to his opposition (Acts 7:2-50; see p. 26)?
2. Stephen trusted God and _____ his enemies (see p. 27).
3. What person is affected by the godliness of Christ in Matthew 27:54 (see p. 27)?
4. A believer's conduct affects the way unbelievers respond to the _____ (see p. 27).
5. What does "institution" refer to in 1 Peter 2:13 (see p. 28)?
6. Why are we to submit to every level of leadership in government (see p. 29)?
7. What is the primary function of civil authority (1 Pet. 2:14; see p. 30)?
8. Civil authorities are _____ of _____ who bear arms to punish evildoers (Rom. 13:4; see p. 30).
9. What is the positive duty of civil authorities (Rom. 13:3; see p. 30)?
10. What do "ignorance" and "foolish" mean in 1 Peter 2:15 (see p. 30)?
11. What does 1 Peter 2:15 teach about God's will (see p. 30)?
12. According to Titus 3:1-2 how is the church to behave toward civil authorities (see p. 30)?

13. Spiritual leaders are not to be _____ (Titus 1:6; see p. 30).
14. What is often the basis of the believer's reputation before the lost (see p. 30)?
15. We are not to use our liberty in Christ as a _____ for sin (see p. 31).
16. According to Proverbs 24:21-22 who will afflict the rebellious and disobedient (see p. 32)?

Pondering the Principles

1. Puritan Richard Baxter said, "Consider how great a crime it is, for a worm to usurp the authority of God, and censure him for not doing justice, and to presume to anticipate his judgment, and take the sword as it were out of his hands, as all do that will be their own avengers. It is the magistrate, and not you, that beareth the sword of public justice; and what he doth not, God will do in his time and way. . . . He that becometh a revenger for himself, doth by his actions as it were say to God, Thou art unjust, and dost not do me justice, and therefore I will do it for myself" (*The Practical Works of Richard Baxter*, vol. 1 [Ligonier, Pa.: Soli Deo Gloria, 1990], p. 783). Don't be a troublemaker. Instead, obey God's Word by being an evangelistic light of godliness (Matt. 5:14-16).

2. Both Stephen and Christ exemplified godliness in unjust situations. Meditate on the following verses. They will help you follow the example of Stephen and Christ and respond to injustice in a biblical way.

   • 1 Samuel 24:3-19

   • Job 31:29-30

   • Psalm 35:11-14

   • Proverbs 20:22; 24:29; 25:21

   • Matthew 5:43-48

   • Romans 12:17-21

   • 1 Thessalonians 5:15

   • 1 Peter 3:13-18

4

Submission in the Workplace—Part 1

Outline

Introduction
A. The Attitude of Society
B. The Example of David
C. The Responsibility of Believers

Lesson
I.   The Mandate for Submission (v. 18)
A. A Slave in Roman Society
B. A Slave in the Early Church
   1. His fear of God
   2. His respect for leaders
      a) The teaching of Peter
      b) The example of Paul
II. The Motive for Submission (v. 19*a*)

Conclusion

Introduction

First Peter 2:18-21 says, "Servants, be submissive to your masters with all respect, not only to those who are good and gentle, but also to those who are unreasonable. For this finds favor, if for the sake of conscience toward God a man bears up under sorrows when suffering unjustly. For what credit is there if, when you sin and are harshly treated, you endure it with patience? But if when you do what is right and suffer for it you patiently endure it, this finds favor with God. For you have been called for this purpose." Those verses tell the believer how to live in society.

A. The Attitude of Society

Our society is preoccupied with demanding its rights. It campaigns for the rights of students, women, children, homosexuals, illegal immigrants, criminals, employees, and the homeless. When people believe their rights have been denied, they often react with strikes, protests, insurrections, and walkouts. The underlying mentality is, "Give me my rights, or I'll fight back in every way possible."

In contrast, God's Word says Christians are not to demand their rights by being troublemakers or lawbreakers in society. The believing citizen is to submit to civil authorities (1 Pet. 2:13-17), and the believing servant is to submit to his master (vv. 18-21).

B. The Example of David

David was an example of how we are to serve others without demanding our rights.

1. His adversary

God chose David to replace Saul as king of Israel. Saul became jealous of David and sought to kill him.

After David killed Goliath, "the women came out of all the cities of Israel, singing and dancing, to meet King Saul, with tambourines, with joy and with musical instruments. And the women sang as they played, and said, 'Saul has slain his thousands, and David his ten thousands.' Then Saul became very angry, for this saying displeased him; and he said, 'They have ascribed to David ten thousands, but to me they have ascribed thousands. Now what more can he have but the kingdom?' And Saul looked at David with suspicion from that day on.

"Now it came about on the next day that an evil spirit from God came mightily upon Saul, and he raved in the midst of the house, while David was playing the harp with his hand, as usual; and a spear was in Saul's hand. And Saul hurled the spear for he thought, 'I will pin David to the wall.' But David escaped from his presence twice" (1 Sam. 18:6-11). He finally had to run away from Saul altogether (19:9-10).

2. His attitude

Even though he knew God had chosen him to be king, David didn't demand his right to rule or seek vengeance against Saul.

a) 1 Samuel 24:2-12—Saul continued to seek David's life. He "took three thousand chosen men from all Israel, and went to seek David and his men in front of the Rocks of the Wild Goats. And he came to the sheepfolds on the way, where there was a cave; and Saul went in to relieve himself.

"Now David and his men were sitting in the inner recesses of the cave. And the men of David said to him, 'Behold, this is the day of which the Lord said to you, "Behold; I am about to give your enemy into your hand, and you shall do to him as it seems good to you."' Then David arose and cut off the edge of Saul's robe secretly.

"And it came about afterward that David's conscience bothered him because he had cut off the edge of Saul's robe. So he said to his men, 'Far be it from me because of the Lord that I should do this thing to my lord, the Lord's anointed, to stretch out my hand against him, since he is the Lord's anointed.' And David persuaded his men with these words and did not allow them to rise up against Saul. And Saul arose, left the cave, and went on his way.

"Now afterward David arose and went out of the cave and called after Saul, saying, 'My lord the king!' And when Saul looked behind him, David bowed with his face to the ground and prostrated himself. And David said to Saul, 'Why do you listen to the words of men, saying, "Behold, David seeks to harm you"? Behold, this day your eyes have seen that the Lord had given you today into my hand in the cave, and some said to kill you, but my eye had pity on you; and I said, "I will not stretch out my hand against my lord, for he is the Lord's anointed."

"'Now, my father, see! Indeed, see the edge of your robe in my hand! For in that I cut off the edge of your robe and did not kill you, know and perceive that there is no evil or rebellion in my hands, and I have not sinned against you, though you are lying in wait for my life to take it. May the Lord judge between you and me. . . . But my hand shall not be against you.'"

b) 1 Samuel 26:6-12—David asked, "'Who will go down with me to Saul in the camp?' And Abishai said, 'I will go down with you.' So David and Abishai came to the people by night, and behold, Saul lay sleeping inside the circle of the camp, with his spear stuck in the ground at his head; and Abner and the people were lying around him. Then Abishai said to David, 'Today God has delivered your enemy into your hand; now therefore, please let me strike him with the spear to the ground with one stroke, and I will not strike him the second time.'

"But David said to Abishai, 'Do not destroy him, for who can stretch out his hand against the Lord's anointed and be without guilt?' David also said, 'As the Lord lives, surely the Lord will strike him, or his day will come that he dies, or he will go down into battle and perish. The Lord forbid that I should stretch out my hand against the Lord's anointed; but now please take the spear that is at his head and the jug of water, and let us go.'

"So David took the spear and the jug of water from beside Saul's head, and they went away, but no one saw or knew it, nor did any awake, for they were all asleep, because a sound sleep from the Lord had fallen on them."

C. The Responsibility of Believers

Believers are to follow David's example of respecting those in authority.

1. Romans 12:17-19—"Never pay back evil for evil to anyone. Respect what is right in the sight of all men. If possible, so far as it depends on you, be at peace with all men. Never take your own revenge, beloved, but leave room for the wrath of God."

2. Luke 6:32-35—"If you love those who love you, what credit is that to you? For even sinners love those who

love them. And if you do good to those who do good to you, what credit is that to you? For even sinners do the same thing. And if you lend to those from whom you expect to receive, what credit is that to you? Even sinners lend to sinners, in order to receive back the same amount. But love your enemies, and do good, and lend, expecting nothing in return; and your reward will be great, and you will be sons of the Most High; for He Himself is kind to ungrateful and evil men."

3. 1 Corinthians 7:20-21, 24—"Let each man remain in that condition in which he was called. Were you called while a slave? Do not worry about it; but if you are able also to become free, rather do that. . . . Let each man remain with God in that condition in which he was called." Although the obvious assumption is that freedom is better than slavery, Paul certainly wasn't calling slaves to rebel against their owners.

Similarly, 1 Peter 2:18-21 says the servant is to submit to his master. Today that implies that the employee is to respect his employer.

Lesson

I. THE MANDATE FOR SUBMISSION (v. 18)

"Servants, be submissive to your masters with all respect, not only to those who are good and gentle, but also to those who are unreasonable."

A. A Slave in Roman Society

The dominant social structure of the Roman Empire was slavery. Often slaves were the objects of disrespect. The influential philosopher Aristotle, for example, implied that friendship and justice are no more applicable to a slave than to a horse or ox. He said, "A slave is a living tool, and a tool is an inanimate slave," reducing the slave even lower—to the level of an inanimate object (*Ethics*, 1161*b*). The Roman nobleman Varro, writing about agriculture, said the only difference between a slave, a beast, and a cart was that a slave could talk (*On Landed Estates*, 1:17.1).

B. A Slave in the Early Church

It's likely that most Christians in the early church were slaves, for 1 Corinthians 1:26-29 says, "Consider your calling, brethren, that there were not many wise according to the flesh, not many mighty, not many noble; but God has chosen the foolish things of the world to shame the wise, and God has chosen the weak things of the world to shame the things which are strong, and the base things of the world and the despised, God has chosen, the things that are not, that He might nullify the things that are, that no man should boast before God." Although many believers had a life of servitude, they were spiritually free in Christ (Gal. 3:28).

In 1 Peter 2:18 the Greek term translated "servants" (*oiketēs*) means "house servants." Most slaves served the owner in his home or estate. "Masters" (*despotēs*, from which we derive the English word *despot*) refers to absolute ownership and power. "Be submissive" speaks of continual submission.

1. His fear of God

   Verse 18 says servants were to submit "with all respect" (Gk., *phobos*, from which we derive the English word *phobia*). The word speaks of fearing God, not man. We are to be mindful of God in what we do and say (1:17; 2:17; 3:2, 15). That includes respecting the social order, such as the employer-employee relationship, since He has sovereignly designed it for the sake of orderliness and productivity.

2. His respect for leaders

   a) The teaching of Peter

   Peter instructed servants to submit to their masters, some of whom were "good and gentle" (2:18). The Greek term translated "good" (*agathos*) refers to kindness and benevolence. "Gentle" (*epieikeia*) speaks of being reasonable and fair. It characterizes someone who willingly forgoes his rights and accepts less than he is due. It's easy to obey someone like that.

   The challenge, Peter implied, is in submitting to those who are "unreasonable" (Gk., *skolios*, from which we derive the English word *scoliosis*). The word means "crooked" or "perverse" and characterizes someone who is harsh, unkind, or ungracious. In our society a person can look for another job if his or her employer is unreasonable. In Peter's day, however, that was not an option, since masters owned their slaves.

b) The example of Paul

While in prison, Paul led Onesimus, a runaway slave, to faith in Christ and sent him back to Philemon, his owner (Philem. 1:10-15). Note that Paul didn't tell Onesimus to give Philemon a difficult time or be an insurrectionist. Rather, his teaching squares with what Peter taught: "Slaves, obey your earthly masters with respect and fear, and with sincerity of heart, just as you would obey Christ. . . .

"Serve wholeheartedly, as if you were serving the Lord, not men, because you know that the Lord will reward everyone for whatever good he does, whether he is slave or free. And masters, treat your slaves in the same way. Do not threaten them, since you know that he who is both their Master and yours is in heaven, and there is no favoritism with him" (Eph. 6:5, 7-9, NIV).

Because God has sovereignly established the social order, we are to serve our employer as though we were serving the Lord (cf. Col. 3:17, 22-25). If employers are unfair, God will deal with them. The mandate is to submit, not to strike or to demonstrate. That doesn't mean such actions are always wrong for employees since strikes and demonstrations are legal provisions in our society, but the overarching principle is to entrust ourselves to God's care, knowing that He will reward us for our willingness to show the proper respect.

II. THE MOTIVE FOR SUBMISSION (v. 19*a*)

"This finds favor."

We please God when we submit to our employer with respect but displease Him when we complain bitterly or are cantankerous. Ephesians 6:6 says we are to work "not by way of eyeservice, as men-pleasers, but as slaves of Christ, doing the will of God from the heart." We are to work hard and have a good attitude, even when the supervisor is not watching. That kind of testimony will not only rebuke the unreasonable person but will also shine as an ornament of God's grace.

Conclusion

When I was a boy, my father told me about a young soldier who had a difficult time in training camp because he was weak physically. One day he was unable to continue a training exercise and lay prone on the ground. The sergeant approached him and kicked him again and again with his boots. The soldier was in such pain that he had to be carried back to his bunk.

When reveille blew the next morning, the sergeant awakened and reached down to put his boots on. As he did, he noticed that someone had shined them. Upon discovering that the young soldier was responsible, he asked why he had done it. The soldier replied, "Because Christ has given me a love for you." The soldier then had an opportunity to give his testimony, and later the sergeant became a Christian.

God's mandate is that we respect and obey those in authority over us. Our attitude should reflect a willingness to endure anything in this life for the joy of the life to come and the opportunity to be a good testimony to others.

Focusing on the Facts

1. What was David's attitude toward Saul (1 Sam. 24:2-12; 26:6-12; see pp. 37-38)?
2. Romans 12:17 says, "_____ pay back evil for evil to anyone" (see p. 38).
3. According to Luke 6:35, who is kind to ungrateful and evil men (see pp. 38-39)?
4. How does the teaching regarding the master and servant in 1 Peter 2:18-21 apply today (see p. 39)?
5. What was the dominant social structure of the Roman Empire (see p. 39)?
6. What does Galatians 3:28 teach (see p. 40)?
7. What does "with all respect" speak of in 1 Peter 2:18 (see p. 40)?
8. Who designs the social order (see p. 40)?

9. What do "good" and "gentle" refer to (1 Pet. 2:18; see p. 40)?

10. What kind of person does "unreasonable" characterize (1 Pet. 2:18; see pp. 40-41)?

11. What does Paul's example in the book of Philemon show us (see p. 41)?

12. According to Ephesians 6:8, what does the Lord reward (see p. 41)?

13. What is the overarching principle for the employee to follow in the workplace (see p. 41)?

14. How do we please God according to 1 Peter 2:18-19 (see p. 41)?

15. What kind of testimony shines as an ornament of God's grace (see pp. 41-42)?

16. What should our attitude reflect a willingness to do (see p. 42)?

Pondering the Principles

1. Colossians 3:23 says we are to "work heartily, as for the Lord rather than for men." What about you? Do you reflect that attitude in your workplace? Do you respect your employer? Are you faithful and diligent, or are you critical, obstinate, and rude? Are you careful about your use of company time and property? Ask the Lord to help you honor His name where you work. If you are an employer or supervisor, ask the Lord to help you treat the workers in a fair and just way.

2. Bible commentator John Brown wrote, "The unkind, irritating behaviour of the master, is not to be sustained as an excuse for evading or disobeying his commands, or even for yielding a grudging obedience: the hardships of the situations are to be patiently submitted to while they continue; and there is to be no attempt to lessen or remove them by neglecting or violating relative duty" (*Expository Discourses on 1 Peter* [Carlisle, Pa.: Banner of Truth Trust, 1975], p. 499). If you are treated unfairly, realize that your obedient service honors Christ and attracts the lost to Him. In addition, the Lord will reward you for it (Eph. 6:8). Read and meditate on Psalm 57, making note of the principles that apply to your situation.

5

Submission in the Workplace—Part 2

Outline

Introduction
A. Spiritual Warfare
B. Godly Behavior

Review
I.   The Mandate for Submission (v. 18)
II. The Motive for Submission (vv. 19-21*a*)

Lesson
A. God's Presence (v. 19)
B. God's Pleasure (v. 20)
C. God's Purpose (v. 21*a*)
III. The Model of Submission (vv. 21*b*-23)

Introduction

A. Spiritual Warfare

God's Word reveals that the world is a battleground. It is the arena of spiritual warfare.

1. Genesis 3:15—The Lord said to the serpent, "I will put enmity between you and the woman, and between your seed and her seed; He shall bruise you on the head, and you shall bruise him on the heel." That specifies the conflict between Satan and Christ, the seed of the woman.

2. Daniel 10:12-13—An angel said, "Do not be afraid, Daniel, for from the first day that you set your heart on understanding this and on humbling yourself before your God, your words were heard, and I have come in response to your words. But the prince of the kingdom of Persia was withstanding me for twenty-one days; then behold, Michael, one of the chief princes, came to help me, for I had been left there with the kings of Persia." God's angels were battling Satan's demons.

3. Ephesians 6:12—"Our struggle is not against flesh and blood, but against the rulers, against the powers, against the world forces of this darkness, against the spiritual forces of wickedness in the heavenly places." God's servants are in conflict with Satan's forces.

4. John 8:44—Christ said to the Pharisees, "You are of your father the devil, and you want to do the desires of your father." Christ made a clear distinction between the children of God and the children of the devil. There is inevitable conflict between the two.

5. John 15:18-19—Christ said to His disciples, "If the world hates you, you know that it has hated Me before it hated you. If you were of the world, the world would love its own; but because you are not of the world, but I chose you out of the world, therefore the world hates you." The world hates both Christ and His followers.

6. John 16:2-3—Christ gave this warning to His disciples: "An hour is coming for everyone who kills you to think that he is offering service to God. And these things they will do, because they have not known the Father, or Me." In the name of religion the ungodly will persecute God's true children.

Because Satan hates God and believers, he attempts to discredit and destroy the church's testimony. One of his favorite tactics is to parade the scandals of professing believers before the lost. That's because what we do sends a clearer message to others than what we say. Therefore it's vital that we have godly behavior and shine as lights "in the midst of a crooked and perverse generation" (Phil. 2:15).

B. Godly Behavior

The book of 1 Peter calls the believer to godly behavior.

1. 1 Peter 1:6-7—"You have been distressed by various trials, that the proof of your faith, being more precious than gold which is perishable, even though tested by fire, may be found to result in praise and glory and honor at the revelation of Jesus Christ." Trials purge away sin and purify us.

2. 1 Peter 1:14—"As obedient children, do not be conformed to the former lusts which were yours in your ignorance, but like the Holy One who called you, be holy yourselves also in all your behavior."

3. 1 Peter 2:1-2, 9—"Putting aside all malice and all guile and hypocrisy and envy and all slander, like newborn babes, long for the pure milk of the word, that by it you may grow in respect to salvation. . . . You are a chosen race, a royal priesthood, a holy nation, a people for God's own possession, that you may proclaim the excellencies of Him who has called you out of darkness into His marvelous light." We are to hunger for God's Word so we can grow spiritually.

4. 1 Peter 2:12—"Keep your behavior excellent among the Gentiles, so that in the thing in which they slander you as evildoers, they may on account of your good deeds, as they observe them, glorify God in the day of visitation." Godly living attracts the lost to Christ and leads them to salvation.

5. 1 Peter 2:15—"Such is the will of God that by doing right you may silence the ignorance of foolish men." Godly behavior silences the believer's critics and brings them to salvation.

6. 1 Peter 3:1-2—"Wives, be submissive to your own husbands so that even if any of them are disobedient to the word, they may be won without a word by the behavior of their wives, as they observe your chaste and respectful behavior." The believing wife is to win her unbelieving husband to Christ by respecting him and living a pure life.

7. 1 Peter 3:13-16—"Who is there to harm you if you prove zealous for what is good? But even if you should

suffer for the sake of righteousness, you are blessed. And do not fear their intimidation, and do not be troubled, but sanctify Christ as Lord in your hearts, always being ready to make a defense to everyone who asks you to give an account for the hope that is in you, yet with gentleness and reverence; and keep a good conscience so that in the thing in which you are slandered, those who revile your good behavior in Christ may be put to shame." By living a godly life the believer will shame those who falsely accuse him.

8. 1 Peter 4:2—We're not to live "for the lusts of men, but for the will of God." Our behavior is to be in line with God's will.

9. 1 Peter 4:12-16—"Do not be surprised at the fiery ordeal among you, which comes upon you for your testing, as though some strange thing were happening to you; but to the degree that you share the sufferings of Christ, keep on rejoicing; so that also at the revelation of His glory, you may rejoice with exultation. If you are reviled for the name of Christ, you are blessed, because the Spirit of glory and of God rests upon you. By no means let any of you suffer as a murderer, or thief, or evildoer, or a troublesome meddler; but if anyone suffers as a Christian, let him not feel ashamed, but in that name let him glorify God." Our suffering should be for godly living, not wrongdoing.

10. 1 Peter 5:8-10—"Be of sober spirit, be on the alert. Your adversary, the devil, prowls about like a roaring lion, seeking someone to devour. But resist him, firm in your faith, knowing that the same experiences of suffering are being accomplished by your brethren who are in the world. And after you have suffered for a little while, the God of all grace, who called you to His eternal glory in Christ, will Himself perfect, confirm, strengthen and establish you." Whatever our circumstances, we are to be true to Christ.

The book of 1 Peter also says that godly behavior includes a submissive attitude in the workplace.

I. THE MANDATE FOR SUBMISSION (v. 18; see pp. 39-41)

"Servants, be submissive to your masters with all respect, not only to those who are good and gentle, but also to those who are unreasonable."

It's not wrong for you to seek change through the proper channels, but it is wrong to disrespect your employer. Ephesians 6:5-8 describes the servant as showing the right behavior by obeying his master, the right attitude by fearing God, the right commitment by being conscientious in his work, and the right intensity by being diligent. If you work like that, your workplace will be a mission field for evangelizing the lost and building up believers. So don't be angry or discontent, but be faithful and obedient.

II. THE MOTIVE FOR SUBMISSION (vv. 19-21a; see pp. 41-42)

Lesson

A. God's Presence (v. 19)

"This finds favor, if for the sake of conscience toward God a man bears up under sorrows when suffering unjustly."

"This finds favor" can be translated "this is a grace." It refers to what is intrinsically attractive or pleasing to God. When a servant patiently endured harsh treatment to honor God's name, God was pleased. In our day God is pleased when we don't retaliate against an unjust supervisor or employer.

Our "conscience toward God" refers to our general awareness of God's presence and is therefore an incentive for godly conduct. The Greek term translated "bears up" (*hupopherō*) means "to endure"; "sorrows" (*lupē*) refers to physical or mental pain. We are to maintain a good testimony before the lost by enduring mistreatment, confident that God sovereignly controls every situation.

In Peter's day mistreated slaves could not relocate to another workplace, since their masters owned them. They weren't able to join a labor union, consult a vocational counselor, or file a civil suit, as many do in today's society. Their patient endurance was not only a testimony to the power of salvation but also an opportunity to exercise great faith. When the lost see the believer's tranquillity in the midst of a great trial, it will attract them to Christ.

B. God's Pleasure (v. 20)

"What credit is there if, when you sin and are harshly treated, you endure it with patience? But if when you do what is right and suffer for it you patiently endure it, this finds favor with God."

This verse expands on verse 19. "Harshly treated" (Gk., *kolaphizō*) means "to strike with the fist," as our Lord was treated before His crucifixion (Mark 14:65). God is pleased, not when we strike back in vengeance, but when we patiently endure mistreatment for doing right. That is a recurring theme in Scripture.

1. 1 Peter 3:14—"If you should suffer for the sake of righteousness, you are blessed. And do not fear their intimidation, and do not be troubled." God blesses believers who suffer unjustly.

2. 1 Peter 4:14-16—"If you are reviled for the name of Christ, you are blessed, because the Spirit of glory and of God rests upon you. By no means let any of you suffer as a murderer, or thief, or evildoer, or a troublesome meddler; but if anyone suffers as a Christian, let him not feel ashamed, but in that name let him glorify God."

3. Matthew 5:11-12—Jesus said, "Blessed are you when men cast insults at you, and persecute you, and say all kinds of evil against you falsely, on account of Me. Rejoice, and be glad, for your reward in heaven is great."

4. 1 Corinthians 4:11-13—Paul and his associates left us this example: "To this present hour we are both hungry and thirsty, and are poorly clothed, and are roughly treated, and are homeless; and we toil, working with our own hands; when we are reviled, we bless; when we are persecuted, we endure; when we are slandered, we try to conciliate."

C. God's Purpose (v. 21a)

"You have been called for this purpose."

"Called" refers to the call of salvation (cf. 1 Pet. 2:9; 5:10). Part of that call means patiently enduring undeserved punishment. As 2 Timothy 3:12 says, "All who desire to live godly in Christ Jesus will be persecuted." Although being a friend of God makes you an enemy in the world's sight (John 15:18-20), unfair treatment in the workplace should not keep you from being a model employee. If your behavior is not Christlike in the workplace, it sends a message to the lost that your heart is set on earthly things, not on heavenly priorities. Your behavior should reflect your settled conviction that God will supply all your needs according to His riches in glory (Phil. 4:19).

III. THE MODEL OF SUBMISSION (vv. 21b-23)

"Christ also suffered for you, leaving you an example for you to follow in His steps, who committed no sin, nor was any deceit found in His mouth; and while being reviled, He did not revile in return; while suffering, He uttered no threats, but kept entrusting Himself to Him who judges righteously."

Although Christ suffered verbal and physical persecution from His enemies, He did not retaliate. In meekness and humility He committed Himself to God. His response to mistreatment is our "example." The Greek term refers to a writing or drawing that's placed under a sheet and traced. We're to pattern our lives after Christ. That we're to follow in His steps means He has left a line of footprints, or tracks, for us to walk in. As One who patiently endured mistreatment, Christ is the perfect example for us to follow.

Focusing on the Facts

1. What conflict does Genesis 3:15 specify (see p. 45)?
2. What clear distinction does Christ make in John 8:44 (see p. 46)?
3. According to John 15:18-19 whom does the world hate (see p. 46)?
4. What in particular does Satan attempt to discredit and destroy? How and why does he attempt to do that (see p. 46)?
5. What is more precious than gold (1 Pet. 1:6-7; see p. 47)?

6. According to 1 Peter 2:9 why did God choose us to be His people (see p. 47)?
7. What brings shame to those who slander the believer (1 Pet. 3:16; see pp. 47-48)?
8. What is our behavior to be in line with (1 Pet. 4:2; see p. 48)?
9. According to Ephesians 6:5-8 how is the servant to work (see p. 49)?
10. What does "conscience toward God" refer to in 1 Peter 2:19 (see p. 49)?
11. In what particular way are we to maintain a good testimony before the lost (see p. 50)?
12. "If you should suffer for the sake of righteousness, you are _____ " (1 Pet. 3:14; see p. 50).
13. According to Matthew 5:11-12 what is cause for rejoicing (see p. 50)?
14. What is part of our call to salvation (1 Pet. 2:21; see p. 51)?
15. What should our behavior reflect in the workplace (Phil. 4:19; see p. 51)?
16. In what particular way is Christ our perfect example to follow (1 Pet. 2:21-23; see p. 51)?

Pondering the Principles

1. In God's calling us to salvation, we have the privilege of suffering for His name (1 Pet. 2:21). English minister Martyn Lloyd-Jones said, "We are like the school boy who would like to evade certain things, and run away from problems and tests. But we thank God that because he has a larger interest in us and knows what is for our good, he puts us through the disciplines of life—he makes us learn the multiplication table; we are made to struggle with the elements of grammar. Many things that are trials to us are essential that one day we may be found without spot or wrinkle" (*The Miracle of Grace* [Grand Rapids: Baker, 1986], p. 39). When you encounter trials in the workplace, view them as opportunities for spiritual growth and for others to see Christ in you.

2. Believers are to work with an awareness of God's presence. That's an incentive not only for godly behavior, but also for trusting in His sovereign control of every situation. Theologian A. W. Pink wrote, "As [one] sees the apparent defeat of the right, and the triumphing of might and the wrong . . . it seems as though Satan were getting the better of the conflict. But as one looks above, instead of around, there is plainly

visible to the eye of faith a Throne. . . . This then is our confidence—God is on the Throne" (*The Sovereignty of God* [Grand Rapids: Baker, 1930], p. 225). Express your thankfulness to God for sovereignly controlling every situation in your workplace.

6

How to Win Your Unbelieving Spouse

Outline

Introduction

Lesson
I.   The Responsibilities of the Wife (vv. 1-6)
     A. Stated Negatively
        1. She is not to leave her husband
        2. She is not to preach at him
        3. She is not to demand her rights
     B. Stated Positively
        1. She is to be submissive
        2. She is to be faithful
        3. She is to be modest
           a) Outward adornment
           b) Inward adornment
II. The Responsibilities of the Husband (v. 7)
     A. He Is to Be Considerate (v. 7a)
     B. He Is to Be Chivalrous (v. 7b)
     C. He Is to Be Her Companion (v. 7c)

Conclusion

Introduction

First Peter 3:1-7 tells the believer how to win his or her spouse to Christ by fulfilling certain responsibilities. Let's find out what they are.

Lesson

I. THE RESPONSIBILITIES OF THE WIFE (vv. 1-6)

"In the same way, you wives, be submissive to your own husbands so that even if any of them are disobedient to the word, they may be won without a word by the behavior of their wives, as they observe your chaste and respectful behavior. And let not your adornment be merely external—braiding the hair, and wearing gold jewelry, or putting on dresses; but let it be the hidden person of the heart, with the imperishable quality of a gentle and quiet spirit, which is precious in the sight of God. For in this way in former times the holy women also, who hoped in God, used to adorn themselves, being submissive to their own husbands. Thus Sarah obeyed Abraham, calling him lord, and you have become her children if you do what is right without being frightened by any fear."

In the Greek and Roman culture of Peter's day, women were treated with little respect. As long as they lived in their father's house, they were under the Roman law of *patria potestas* (the father's power), which gave fathers the power of life and death over their daughters. Once a woman married, her husband had that same legal power. Women were regarded as mere servants who were to remain indoors and obey their husbands. Since it was socially taboo for women to make their own decisions, their deciding to follow Christ sometimes resulted in severe abuse from their unbelieving husbands. In spite of such difficult circumstances, the believing wife can win her husband to Christ by fulfilling certain responsibilities.

A. Stated Negatively

1. She is not to leave her husband

   First Corinthians 7:13 says that if the unbelieving husband consents to live with his believing wife, she is not to divorce him. In fact, verse 14 says he will benefit from the blessings that God bestows on his wife. However, if he wants to leave, she should let him do so (7:15), since his staying would only produce a chaotic environment.

2. She is not to preach at him

She is not to badger, argue, or harangue him with the gospel. Peter said he "may be won without a word" from her godly behavior. That means she is not to put Bible verses on his beer cans, stick evangelistic tracts under his pillow, or call the pastor to the house to unload the gospel gun!

3. She is not to demand her rights

Although the believing wife is spiritually equal with all other believers, that doesn't negate her responsibility to submit to her husband.

B. Stated Positively

1. She is to be submissive

First Peter 3:1 says, "In the same way, you wives, be submissive to your own husbands so that even if any of them are disobedient to the word, they may be won without a word by the behavior of their wives." "In the same way" refers to the submission of citizens to civil authorities (2:13) and servants to their masters (2:18).

The Greek word translated "be submissive" (*hupotassō*) is a military term that means "to subject" or "rank under." The wife's biblical role is to submit to the leadership of her husband (1 Cor. 11:3; Eph. 5:22-23). In no way does that imply that she is inferior in terms of character, intelligence, or spirituality—just like a commanding officer is not necessarily superior in those terms to the individuals under him, but his authority is essential to complete a given task efficiently. "Be submissive *to your own husbands*" (1 Pet. 3:1, emphasis added) speaks of the intimacy of marriage and also makes clear that women aren't being told to submit to men in general.

"Disobedient to the word" (3:1) characterizes the unbelieving husband who rejects the gospel. His believing wife is to submit to him so that he might be won to Christ "without a word" (v. 1). That doesn't refer to *the* Word of God since that is essential for anyone's salvation (1 Pet. 1:23) but to words that are spoken. The wife is to win her husband to Christ not by what she says but by how she behaves. A lovely, gracious, gentle, submissive attitude is one of the most effective evangelistic tools she has.

2. She is to be faithful

First Peter 3:2 says the godly wife is to have "chaste and respectful behavior." She is to be pure and irreproachable before God and her husband.

3. She is to be modest

Verses 3-6 say, "Let not your adornment be merely external—braiding the hair, and wearing gold jewelry, or putting on dresses; but let it be the hidden person of the heart, with the imperishable quality of a gentle and quiet spirit, which is precious in the sight of God. For in this way in former times the holy women also, who hoped in God, used to adorn themselves, being submissive to their own husbands. Thus Sarah obeyed Abraham, calling him lord, and you have become her children if you do what is right without being frightened by any fear."

a) Outward adornment

Certainly Peter wasn't forbidding women from styling their hair or wearing jewelry and nice clothing. After all, the bride in the book of Song of Solomon was beautifully adorned. It's just that women aren't to be preoccupied with such things. In Roman society there was an immense preoccupation with outward adornment. Women dyed their hair outlandish colors, braided it elaborately, and were fond of expensive jewelry, elegant clothing, and fine cosmetics.

Such a preoccupation wasn't anything new, for the Lord told of coming judgment against the women of Israel by saying He would "take away the beauty of their anklets, headbands, crescent ornaments, dangling earrings, bracelets, veils, headdresses, ankle chains, sashes, perfume boxes, amulets, finger rings, nose rings, festal robes, outer tunics, cloaks, money purses, hand mirrors, undergarments, turbans, and veils. . . . Instead of sweet perfume there will be putrefaction; instead of a belt, a rope; instead of well-set hair, a plucked-out scalp; instead

58

of fine clothes, a donning of sackcloth; and branding instead of beauty" (Isa. 3:18-24).

b) Inward adornment

Instead of making her appearance an all-day affair, the wife's primary focus should be on adorning "the hidden person of the heart" (1 Pet. 3:4). That refers to the true inner beauty of character and virtue. Paul said for Christian women "to adorn themselves with proper clothing, modestly and discreetly, not with braided hair and gold or pearls or costly garments; but rather by means of good works, as befits women making a claim to godliness" (1 Tim. 2:9-10).

The wife is to adorn her inner person "with the imperishable quality of a gentle and quiet spirit" (1 Pet. 3:4). "Gentle" (Gk., *praupathia*) means "meek," "quiet" (*hēsuchios*) means "still" or "tranquil," and "spirit" refers to a person's disposition. A meek and calm disposition characterizes inner beauty and "is precious in the sight of God" (v. 4).

God highly values the inner beauty of godliness, but that's no excuse for outer sloppiness. Underdoing it will draw as much attention to your outward appearance as overdoing it. You've dressed appropriately when your outward appearance simply reflects the inner beauty God has fashioned in you.

Verses 5-6 illustrate what inner beauty is all about: "In this way in former times the holy women also, who hoped in God, used to adorn themselves, being submissive to their own husbands. Thus Sarah obeyed Abraham, calling him lord, and you have become her children if you do what is right without being frightened by any fear."

"Holy women" (v. 5) refers to women described in the Old Testament who were true believers. The principle of wives submitting to their husbands is not something new since that's the example we see in the Old Testament. Verse 6 specifically names Sarah as the model of submission because of her continual obedience to her husband, Abraham, and obvious respect for him. All true believers are children of Abraham by faith (Rom. 4:5-16; Gal. 3:7-

29). Similarly, all believing women who follow Sarah's example of submission are her children.

"Without being frightened by any fear" (1 Pet. 3:6) speaks of intimidation. It seems that every society since the Fall has tried to intimidate women from submitting to their husbands. But instead of being intimidated, the wife is to "do what is right" by being submissive, faithful, and modest. That will help win her husband to Christ.

II. THE RESPONSIBILITIES OF THE HUSBAND (v. 7)

"You husbands likewise, live with your wives in an understanding way, as with a weaker vessel, since she is a woman; and grant her honor as a fellow heir of the grace of life, so that your prayers may not be hindered."

"Likewise" refers to the duty of submission (1 Pet. 2:13, 18; 3:1). Ephesians 5:21 says all believers are to submit to one another, which includes the wife to her husband and vice versa. The husband is to submit in the sense of caring for his wife's needs, which involves a threefold responsibility.

A. He Is to Be Considerate (v. 7a)

"You husbands likewise, live with your wives in an understanding way."

"Understanding" (Gk., *gnōsis*) speaks of being sensitive to the wife's deepest physical and emotional needs. "Live" (Gk., *sunoikeō*) means "to dwell together" and speaks of living with someone in an intimate way. Far from being indifferent to his wife, the husband is to nourish and cherish her in the bond of intimacy (Eph. 5:25-28).

B. He Is to Be Chivalrous (v. 7b)

"As with a weaker vessel, since she is a woman."

"Weaker vessel" refers to the woman's being physically weaker than the man. Because of that, the husband is to protect and provide for her.

C. He Is to Be Her Companion (v. 7c)

"Grant her honor as a fellow heir of the grace of life, so that your prayers may not be hindered."

"Grace of life" refers to marriage, not salvation. "Grace" simply means "a gift," and one of the best gifts that life has to offer is marriage. That's especially true when the husband cultivates companionship and fellowship with his wife. In Greek and Roman society, however, it was common for the husband to expect his wife to clean house and bear children but not enter into a true, intimate friendship with him. In contrast, the Christian husband is to love and respect his wife so his prayers won't be impeded. Since his prayers would include petitions for her salvation, it's important that he develop an intimate friendship with her.

Conclusion

Whether as a citizen, an employee, or a marriage partner, the role of the Christian is always the same: obey God's ordained pattern of submission. Doing so will please God and be a testimony that honors Him before the lost.

Focusing on the Facts

1. What advice does 1 Corinthians 7:13-15 give to the wife (see p. 56)?
2. What does "in the same way" refer to in 1 Peter 3:1 (see p. 57)?
3. What is the wife's biblical role (Eph. 5:22-23; see p. 57)?
4. Who does "disobedient to the word" characterize (1 Pet. 3:1; see p. 57)?
5. What does "without a word" refer to (1 Pet. 3:1; see pp. 57-58)?
6. What is one of the most effective evangelistic tools the wife has (see p. 58)?
7. What does "chaste and respectful behavior" mean (1 Pet. 3:2; see p. 58)?
8. What is the Lord's indictment against the women of Israel in Isaiah 3:18-24 (see pp. 58-59)?
9. What should be the wife's primary focus (1 Pet. 3:4; see p. 59)?
10. What does 1 Timothy 2:9-10 teach (see p. 59)?
11. What characterizes inner beauty? What is God's evaluation of it (1 Pet. 3:4; see p. 59)?

12. Why is Sarah named as the model of submission? In what way are Christian women her children (1 Pet. 4:5-6; see p. 59)?
13. What does Ephesians 5:21 teach? How does that apply to the husband (see p. 60)?
14. What do "understanding" and "live" speak of in 1 Peter 3:7 (see p. 60)?
15. What does Ephesians 5:25-28 teach (see p. 60)?
16. What does "the grace of life" refer to in 1 Peter 3:7? Why is it important for the husband to love and respect his wife (see p. 61)?

Pondering the Principles

1. Complete the following evaluation, asking the Lord to help you improve where necessary as a marriage partner:

   • Study Philippians 2:3-4 and Ephesians 4:1-3, and write out five specific ways to demonstrate to your spouse that he or she is important.

   • Evaluate the changes you would like to see in your mate. Will they truly help your mate, or are they only for your own benefit?

   • List five things you do to please your mate and five things you should do more often.

   • List five deficiencies you have as a marriage partner. Specifically list ways you can change.

2. The wife is to be submissive, faithful, and modest toward her husband; and the husband is to show consideration, chivalry, and companionship toward his wife. Answer the following practical questions as a way of measuring those virtues in your life:

   • Are you faithful to maintain your spiritual life through Bible study, prayer, regular church attendance, and fellowship with God's people?

   • Do you ask forgiveness when you have done something wrong?

   • Do you accept corrective criticisms graciously?

- Do you make excessive demands upon your mate, expecting too much from him or her?

- Do you allow your mate to make mistakes without condemning him or her?

- Do you focus on what you appreciate about your mate, or do you tend to find fault with him or her?

- Can you discuss differing viewpoints without becoming irritated or upset?

- When you disagree with your mate, do you seek biblical answers for the problem instead of blowing up emotionally or verbally attacking your mate?

- Are you a good listener when your mate tries to explain something?

- Do you become irritated over your mate's weaknesses, or do you provide acceptance, encouragement, and a proper example?

If you've spotted some problems in your life, prayerfully seek to make the necessary corrections. To help you in your resolve, seek the counsel and accountability of a godly friend who is a fellow wife or husband.

Scripture Index

Genesis
2:7	11
3:15	45
50:24	13

1 Samuel
2:21-22	13, 32
18:6-11	36
19:9-10	36
24:2-12	37-38
26:6-12	38

Proverbs
24:21	19

Isaiah
3:1-2	28
3:8	28
3:18-24	59
10:3	13
55:11	23

Jeremiah
24:5-7	20
27:22	13
29:6-14	19

Daniel
9:11-12	28-29
10:12-13	46

Micah
7:2-3	29

Matthew
5:11-12	50
5:16	9
11:28-30	21
17:24-27	28
22:21	19
27:54	27

Mark
1:25	30
4:39	30
13:19	28
14:65	50

Luke
1:68	14
6:32-35	38-39
7:16	14
19:44	14
23:34	27

John
6:53	18
8:44	46
15:18-20	46, 51
16:2-3	46
19:15	18

Acts
4:18-20	21-22
5:29	22
6:8-14	26
7:2–8:1	27
16:23-25	22
16:31-34	22
17:6	12
19:21-41	18
26:1-32	29
28:22	12

Romans
1:9-10	29

4:5-16	59
6:22	31
7:14-25	11
8:23	11
12:17-19	38
13:1	29
13:1-7	19-21, 28-29
13:3	30
13:4	30

1 Corinthians
1:26-29	40
4:11-13	50-51
5:1	12
7:20-24	39
7:22	31
10:16	18
11:3	57
12:2	12

2 Corinthians
| 5:17 | 28 |
| 10:3-5 | 12, 22 |

Galatians
3:7-29	60
3:28	40
5:13	31
5:16	12
5:19-21	11

Ephesians
5:21	60
5:22-23	57
5:25-28	60
6:5-9	41-42, 49
6:17	23

Philippians
2:15	46
3:20	10
4:19	51

Colossians
| 3:17 | 41 |
| 3:22-25 | 41 |

1 Timothy
| 2:1-6 | 23 |

2 Timothy
| 3:12 | 51 |

Titus
| 3:1-5 | 30 |

Philemon
| 10-15 | 41 |

Hebrews
| 13:14 | 10 |

James
1:14-15	11
3:9	31
4:1	11

1 Peter
1:1	9
1:6-7	47
1:14	47
1:18-19	31
1:23	57
2:1-2	47
2:2	11
2:5	11
2:9	47, 51
2:9-10	9
2:11	10-12
2:11-12	7-16
2:12	12-15, 27, 47
2:13	17-24, 28, 57, 60
2:13-17	25-34, 27
2:14	12, 30
2:15	8-9, 30, 47
2:16	30-31
2:17	31-32
2:18	38-41, 60

2:18-19	35-44
2:19	41-42, 49-50
2:19-23	45-54
2:20	50-51
2:21	20, 51
2:21-23	51
2:23	20, 27
3:1	10, 57, 60
3:1-2	47
3:1-7	55-64
3:2	58
3:3-6	58-59
3:4	59
3:5	59
3:6	59-60
3:7	60-61
3:13-16	47-48
3:14	50
4:1-3	12
4:2	48
4:12	9
4:12-16	48
4:14-16	50
4:15	12
5:8-10	48
5:10	51

1 John

2:15-17	10

3 John

7	12

Topical Index

Activism, Christian, 29. *See also* Government
Anti-Semitism, in ancient Rome, 17-18
Authority. *See* Government

Barclay, William, on ancient anti-Semitism, 18
Baxter, Richard
on inner discipline, 15-16
on submitting to the government, 33
Behavior, godly. *See* Godliness
Brown, John
on submitting to the government, 24
on submitting to one's master, 43

Citizenship. *See* Government
Civil authority. *See* Government
Clingen, Herb and Ruth, World War II internment of, 14-15
Criticism, silencing worldly, 9, 30
Culver, Robert, on submitting to the government, 20, 24, 29
Cynicism, silencing worldly, 7-64

David, submissiveness of, 36-38
Demonstrations, 36, 41

Discipline, self. *See* Self-Discipline

Employment. *See* Work
Evangelism, action vs. words, 9

God
awareness of, 49, 52-53
sovereignty of, 49, 52-53
visitation by, 13-15
Godliness, 7-18, 47-48
Government
purpose of, 30
rebellion against, 21-22, 36
respect for, 17-34, 36-37
submission to, 17-34

Haldane, Robert, on submitting to the government, 21
Husbands, responsibility of, 55-64

Japanese camp commandant. *See* Konishi
Jesus Christ
example of, 27, 33
submissiveness of, 27, 33

Konishi, Japanese camp commandant, 14-15

Leighton, Robert, on silencing one's critics, 9
Lifestyle, a godly, 7-18
Living. *See* Lifestyle

Maclaren, Alexander, on people's notion of God, 9
Mankind, respect for all, 31
Marriage
  evaluating your, 62-63
  submission in, 55-64
  unbelieving spouse and, 55-64

Pink, A. W., on confidence in God, 52-53

Rebellion, against the government. *See* Government
Respect
  for all mankind, 31
  for authority, 17-34
Rights, preoccupation with, 36

Self-Discipline, 10-12, 15-16
Silencing ungodly critics, 9, 30
Slander, refuting ungodly, 9, 12-18, 30
Slavery, in ancient Rome, 39-41
Soldier who was a godly example to his ungodly sergeant, 42
Soul, defining the, 11
Spiritual warfare. *See* Warfare
Stephen, submissiveness of, 25-27, 33
Striking, 36, 41
Submission
  to civil authority, 17-34
  to one's spouse, 55-64
  in the workplace, 35-54
Suffering, for Christ, 51-52

Taxes, paying one's, 27-28
Testimony, a godly, 42, 46

Unequally yoked, 55-64
Unions, 50. *See also* Striking

Visitation, by God. *See* God

Walkouts, 36, 41
Warfare, spiritual, 22-23, 45-46
"Weaker vessel," 60
Wives, responsibility of, 55-64
Women
  in ancient society, 56, 58
  appearance of, 58-59
  holy, 59-60
  See also Wives
Work
  ethical behavior at, 43
  submission at, 35-54
World, cynicism of the, 7-64
World War II, internment of missionaries by the Japanese, 14-15